9/17

Zoom in on
BRIDGES

Hannah Isbell

Enslow Publishing
101 W. 23rd Street
Suite 240
New York, NY 10011
USA

enslow.com

WORDS TO KNOW

abutment The structure at the ends of a bridge that holds much of the bridge's weight.

beam The part of a beam bridge that stretches from one end to the other.

compression The force caused by objects being pushed together.

deck The part of a suspension bridge that carries traffic.

engineer Someone who designs, builds, or works with machines and structures.

force Strength or energy.

load The weight a bridge must support.

obstacle A barrier.

pier The support of a beam bridge.

span The length of a bridge.

tension The force caused by stretching an object.

torsion The force caused by twisting the ends of an object in opposite directions.

CONTENTS

The Brooklyn Bridge is one of the most famous bridges in the world.

Overcoming Obstacles

A bridge is a perfect example of human creativity and problem solving. Every bridge in the world marks a place where people ran into an obstacle and figured out how to overcome it. Problem solving is one of the most important parts of being an engineer.

Early People on the Go

The first humans were always moving. They traveled in groups searching for food. Later, people settled in villages and cities. They traveled between places to trade goods and ideas. Today we still move our things and ourselves from place to place, but sometimes obstacles like rivers and canyons stand in our way.

A river might be too wide to swim across. It might be too violent and rocky for a boat. A lake might be too large to go

Still Standing

The oldest bridge in the world is the Arkadiko Bridge in Greece. It dates back to the thirteenth century BCE, making it at least fifteen thousand years old!

The Mississippi River is very wide. Many bridges have been built to cross this large river.

around. A canyon can be too deep to cross. Bridges make people's journeys safer and faster, and people have been building them for at least fifteen thousand years!

The First Bridges

The first bridges were probably fallen trees laid across small obstacles like streams. This type of bridge is called a beam bridge. It is made of a beam that is held up at each end by supports called piers.

These early bridges could not hold much weight. The load, or weight the bridge had to support, put pressure on the beam. This pressure caused a force called compression.

For small gaps, this wasn't too much of a problem. The piers could help support the load. But wider gaps meant

In the first bridges, the fallen tree acted as the beam, and the land on either side of the obstacle, like the banks of a stream, acted as the piers.

that the beam had to do more work. If the load was too heavy, it would start to bend in the middle. After a while, it would buckle, or collapse, from the compression. People had to build better bridges!

Problems and Solutions

Compression is one of the forces engineers have to think about when they build bridges. The thicker a beam is, the more compression it can handle. Early bridge builders tied logs together to make the beam stronger. Later, they began using sturdier materials like stone and steel. But no matter how thick a beam is, compression can still push it down in the middle. Heavier materials also make the bridge itself heavier and could cause it to collapse under its own weight.

The Lake Pontchartrain Causeway is one of the longest bridges in the world. It is called a viaduct because it is made of many smaller sections.

One way to make beam bridges longer is to add more piers and beams, connecting small bridges together into one big one. This is called a viaduct. The extra supports keep a viaduct from buckling.

Arches

Another way to stop a bridge from buckling is to take some of the pressure off the middle of the beam. Ancient engineers solved this problem

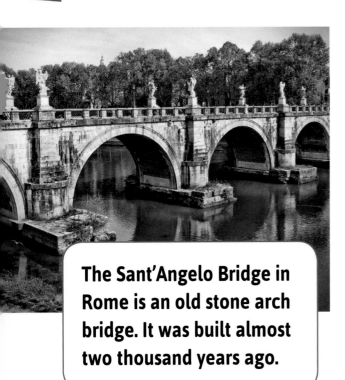

The Sant'Angelo Bridge in Rome is an old stone arch bridge. It was built almost two thousand years ago.

by designing arch bridges. The shape of the arch pushes the pressure away from the middle of the bridge and toward abutments on either side. This design meant bridges could be made of stronger, heavier materials like stone.

Built to Last

The ancient Romans were famous for building bridges. They used strong stone and careful planning and design. Their bridges were so strong that many of them survive to this day!

Trusses

Engineers can also take pressure off the beam by adding a truss. A truss is made of metal or wood arranged into triangles. It helps support the deck, the part of the bridge that carries traffic. A truss can be built above the deck, or below the deck.

Suspension Bridges

Another early type of bridge was made of ropes. People used strong plant material like vines and reeds. They hung them on each side of the obstacle. This type of bridge is called a suspension bridge because "suspend" is another word for "hanging." The earliest suspension bridges were very simple. Sometimes they were just two or three ropes that people could hold onto for balance.

Girls walk on a rope bridge through the forest. Many early bridges were hanging, or suspension, bridges like this.

These simple suspension bridges could have long spans, so they could cover wide gaps. But they weren't very strong or stable. To make these rope bridges more stable, people began tying together pieces of bamboo or planks of wood.

Woven Bridges

Rope bridges are still used today. Many ropes can be woven together to make the bridge safer and stronger.

tower

deck

cables

The Verrazano-Narrows Bridge in New York City. Notice the suspension bridge's tall tower, cables, and deck.

Longer and Stronger

A little over two hundred years ago, people began using iron and steel to build bridges. These materials are stronger and more flexible than stone. In modern suspension bridges, steel cables are used instead of ropes. The cables hang from towers. They use tension, the pulling force, to hold up the deck.

In modern suspension bridges, the cables, towers, and supports on either side of the bridge all help to support the load. This makes suspension bridges very strong. Not only are they able to have long spans, but they can carry more traffic. They can even have more than one deck, for more cars, trains, and people.

One of the most famous bridge collapses was caused in part by torsion. In 1940, the Tacoma Narrows Bridge opened. It quickly became famous for swaying and vibrating in the wind. It was nicknamed Galloping Gertie. It collapsed only a few months after it was built, when the wind caused it to twist and fall apart.

Building Better Bridges

Sometimes there are problems with suspension bridges. High winds can cause torsion, the twisting force. Torsion happens when the two ends of an object are twisted in opposite directions. When you wring out a washcloth, you are applying torsion. When torsion acts on a bridge, it can cause the bridge to break apart.

Engineers must think about torsion and all the forces that will act on a bridge when they are designing it.

The Golden Gate Bridge is famous for its beautiful design. It has been declared one of the Wonders of the Modern World.

Works of Art

Over the thousands of years people have been building bridges, there have been many different designs. When building bridges, engineers think about how long a bridge must be, what kind of traffic it must support, and the forces that will act on it.

Engineers also think about how a bridge will look. They try to make bridges that are beautiful and that fit into their natural surroundings. Bridges are not only useful, but can be works of art!

Engineers work hard to make sure bridges are safe.

21

ACTIVITY
BUILD A BRIDGE CHALLENGE!

You will need:

- *paper*
- *tape*
- *ruler*
- *two platforms (desks, boxes, or stacks of books) of equal height placed one foot apart*
- *water bottle*
- *two or more groups*

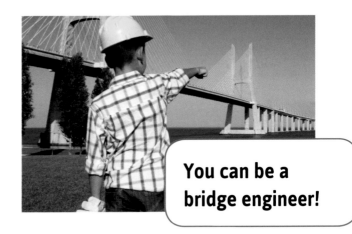

You can be a bridge engineer!

Challenge:

Using only ten pieces of paper per group, try to build a bridge that can span a one-foot (thirty centimeter) gap and support a full water bottle! You may roll, fold, and cut the paper any way you like.

Step 1: Design the bridge.

Study the different types of bridges in this book and decide on a basic design. Will you make a beam bridge, an arch bridge, a truss bridge, or a suspension bridge?

Step 2: Build your bridge.

Fold, roll, cut, and tape your papers to build your bridge. Be creative and don't be afraid to mess up!

Step 3: Test the bridge.

Place each end of the bridge on desks or boxes that are one-foot (thirty centimeter) apart. Fill a water bottle halfway and close the lid. Place the bottle in the middle of the bridge. If the bridge can support the bottle, add more water to see how much weight it will hold!

This activity is great for teams to engage in friendly competition! See what different bridge designs you and your friends and classmates can come up with!

LEARN MORE

Books

Finger, Brad. *13 Bridges Children Should Know.* New York, NY: Prestel, 2015.

Hoena, Blake. *Building the Golden Gate Bridge.* N. Mankato, MN: Capstone Press, 2014.

Stine, Megan. *Where Is the Brooklyn Bridge?* New York, NY: Grosset & Dunlap, 2016.

Websites

All About Bridges: Importance and Types
easyscienceforkids.com/all-about-bridges/
Includes fun facts about bridges plus video and photos.

Building Big: Bridges
www.pbs.org/wgbh/buildingbig/bridge/index.html
Learn about types of bridges and famous bridges and take a bridge challenge!

INDEX

Published in 2018 by Enslow Publishing, LLC.
101 W. 23rd Street, Suite 240, New York, NY 10011

Library of Congress Cataloging-in-Publication Data

Names: Isbell, Hannah, author.
Title: Zoom in on bridges / Hannah Isbell.
Description: New York : Enslow Publishing, [2018] | Series: Zoom in on engineering | Includes bibliographical references and index. | Audience: Grades K-3.
Identifiers: LCCN 2017003014| ISBN 9780766087248 (library-bound) | ISBN 9780766088375 (pbk.) | ISBN 9780766088313 (6-pack)
Subjects: LCSH: Bridges—Juvenile literature. | Bridges—Design and construction—Juvenile literature.
Classification: LCC TG148 .I83 2018 | DDC 624.2—dc23
LC record available at https://lccn.loc.gov/2017003014

Printed in the United States of America

To Our Readers: We have done our best to make sure all website addresses in this book were active and appropriate when we went to press. However, the author and the publisher have no control over and assume no liability for the material available on those websites or on any websites they may link to. Any comments or suggestions can be sent by e-mail to customerservice@enslow.com.

Photo Credits: Cover, pp. 1 (inset), 4 dibrova/Shutterstock.com; cover, p. 1 (background) 8010116134/Shutterstock.com; pp. 5, 10, 14, 19 DWGrafix/DigitalVision Vectors/Getty Images; hoto Image/Shutterstock.com; p. 9 Michael DeYoung/Perspectives/Getty Images; p. 11 Matthew D White/Photolibrary/Getty Images; p. 12 Tupungato/Shutterstock.com; p. 15 Gen Umekita/Moment/Getty Images; p. 16 John Cardasis/Photographers Choice RF/Getty Images; p. 18 Bettmann/Getty Images; p. 20 narvikk/E+/Getty Images; p. 21 Zigy Kaluzny-Charles Thatcher/The Image Bank/Getty Images; p. 22 pjcross/Shutterstock.com; graphic elements (red arc) Lucky Team Studio/Shutterstock.com.